$\mathcal{R}$.s.v.p.

Nobody hands out invitations to their ow[n] [...] asks whether we want to be born. But h[...] book we're about to read asks us to see life as more than just 'being alive'. In the pages of John's Gospel, we meet an extraordinary person — Jesus. And it's Jesus who gives us the invitation to attend our own new birth. It's an invitation to live as God wants us to live — living life to the full. Like most invitations, it has an R.S.V.P. Those four letters stand for the French, *Répondez s'il vous plaît* — 'Please reply'. It's up to us to say 'yes' or 'no'. Through reading John's book, many people have said 'yes' to this invitation, 'yes' to new life with Jesus. We pray you'll want to say it too.

discovering jesus in john's gospel

ℳAKING THE MOST OF THIS BOOK

What's in it?

RSVP guides you through 25 selections from one of the books of the Bible. Usually called 'John', it is one of four Gospels in the New Testament section of the Bible. The word 'gospel' means message, often a good news message. RSVP explores the good news about Jesus Christ, as told by John. We suggest you work through one page of RSVP each day. For your convenience we've included the relevant Bible text each day. For each of the 25 selections, RSVP offers some comments which help you see the point John is making. To continue on from what you have learned in RSVP, we strongly recommend you purchase your own copy of the Bible in a modern translation such as the *Contemporary English Version* used here or the *Good News Bible*.

John who?

The writer of this Gospel was probably the fisherman John, son of Zebedee. He calls himself 'Jesus' favourite disciple' (John 13:23; 19:26; 21:7; 21:20). He wasn't suggesting Jesus didn't love the other disciples. He may have been trying to hide his identity or letting us know this was a first hand account from one of Jesus' closest friends. John was there and saw with his own eyes the things Jesus did. (See John 21:24.)

Finding your way

When we refer to the Bible here, we include the book of the Bible, the chapter, and the verses. For example: John 1:1-15 means the Gospel of John, chapter 1, verses 1 to 15. Numbers in brackets refer to the verses in the passage you are reading. For example: (8) means see verse 8 in the passage. To find the particular book, look up the Contents page found at the beginning of your Bible.

You can use RSVP in a group, or by yourself, or a combination of both methods.

Together or alone?

If you're alone, try to find a quiet place to read and pray. It's helpful to have a regular time too. A notebook and pen will come in handy for jotting down things you discover. If you're with a group, you'll need a suitable place and time to meet. One way to combine both is to read individually each day, and meet weekly as a group to compare what each of you has learned. You could meet weekly for five weeks and cover five readings each time you meet.

To help with group meetings, you'll find a group question — 'Talk Together' — with each day's reading. There are more ideas for groups on page 5.

Share with someone

If you can't meet in a group, it's important to have someone to talk to about these things. It may be the person who gave you this copy of RSVP or someone from your local church. Don't be shy! We learn best by asking questions and sharing thoughts. You can't easily do it all on your own — Christianity isn't for 'lone rangers'!

Whether you're by yourself or with a group, these four steps will help you as you read.

FOUR STEPS

1. Prepare.
Ask God to help you understand the Bible passage.

2. Read.
Read the Bible verses for the day.

3. Explore.
Before you read the RSVP comments, think about what you have learned from the Bible verses. Then read the comments in RSVP and write down any important discoveries that you want to remember.

4. Respond.
Ask God to help you to make what you've learned a part of your life. Ask for assistance to put this into practice.

Beginning with Jesus

You may have only just begun to be a Christian, or you may be wondering how to take the first step. Pages 60 and 61 offer a simple and clear explanation.

TALK TOGETHER

Suggestions for your group

Exploring the Bible with a group can lead to all sorts of exciting discoveries. There are many methods you can use. Here's one. It fits the material covered in this RSVP book.

1. Before each meeting of the group, decide which RSVP readings you will cover. We recommend that you arrange five weekly meetings and cover five readings at each meeting.

2. Agree together that you will all write down your responses to the 'Talk Together' question for each reading.

3. If members of your group do not know each other, allow time for building relationships. There are many books on small groups which offer help in this area.*

4. Ask each other whether there are any parts of the week's reading which have been puzzling. List these puzzles and seek answers together. If necessary ask for help from an experienced leader or allow time for further study during the week.

5. Compare notes. Work through some of the 'Talk Together' questions and compare responses in the group.

6. Finally allow time for group members to share something that God is doing in their lives. Pray for each other.

* For help and ideas in all aspects of small groups, read *Growing Christians in small groups* by John Mallison (Scripture Union UK/Open Book), sold in most Christian bookshops.

discovering
jesus in
john's gospel

1 ¹ In the beginning was the one who is called the Word.
The Word was with God and was truly God.
² From the very beginning the Word was with God.

³ And with this Word, God created all things.
Nothing was made without the Word.
Everything that was created
⁴ received its life from him,
and his life gave light to everyone.
⁵ The light keeps shining in the dark,
and darkness has never put it out.
⁶ God sent a man named John,
⁷ who came to tell about the light
and to lead all people to have faith.
⁸ John wasn't that light.
He came only to tell about the light.

JOHN 1:1-15

⁹ The true light that shines on everyone
was coming into the world.
¹⁰ The Word was in the world,
but no one knew him,
though God had made the world with his Word.
¹¹ He came into his own world,
but his own nation did not welcome him.
¹² Yet some people accepted him
and put their faith in him.
So he gave them the right to be the children of God.
¹³ They were not God's children by nature
or because of any human desires.
God himself was the one
who made them his children.

¹⁴ The Word became a human being
and lived here with us.
We saw his true glory,

the glory of the only Son of the Father.
From him all the kindness and all the truth of God
have come down to us.

¹⁵ John spoke about him and shouted, "This is the
one I told you would come! He is greater than I am,
because he was alive before I was born."

1. WHO'S IT ALL ABOUT?

John gives his book a big start: he describes in pictorial
language the birth of the universe! Jesus Christ is there with
God, calling the whole universe into being (3-4 and 10).

1. More than a human? One of the central facts of the
Christian faith is that God actually became a human being (14).

Many people admire Jesus as a good man or a great teacher. But
John sees there is much more to Jesus than this. Jesus was fully
human (14), but he also *was* and *is* God (1), the same God who
made the beauty of the stars, the complexity of the human
brain and created the joy of friendship.

2. A choice. This world has its beauties — and its dark side
too. Jesus is a light in that darkness (5,9). Each of us faces a
choice. Do we prefer darkness or light? If we choose Jesus, we
become God's children (12) and we are given a new start.
Sadly, many fail to make that choice. Even some of Jesus' own
people did not accept him (11).
So Jesus knows what it's like to be human, to be
rejected as all of us are sometimes.

Prayer: Thank you God that you created this marvellous
universe through your Son, Jesus. Thank you that you cared
enough about us to send him to be one of us. Amen.

TALK TOGETHER

*Talk about some
of the things in
creation that
you love.
Thank Jesus for
making them.*

2

35The next day, John was there again, and two of his followers were with him. 36When he saw Jesus walking by, he said, "Here is the Lamb of God!" 37John's two followers heard him, and they went with Jesus.

38When Jesus turned and saw them, he asked, "What do you want?"

They answered, "Rabbi, where do you live?" The Hebrew word "Rabbi'" means "Teacher."

JOHN 1: 35-51

39Jesus replied, "Come and see!" It was already about four o'clock in the afternoon when they went with him and saw where he lived. So they stayed on for the rest of the day.

40One of the two men who had heard John and had gone with Jesus was Andrew, the brother of Simon Peter. 41The first thing Andrew did was to find his brother and tell him, "We have found the Messiah!" The Hebrew word "Messiah" means the same as the Greek word "Christ."

42Andrew brought his brother to Jesus. And when Jesus saw him, he said, "Simon son of John, you will be called Cephas." This name can be translated as "Peter."

43-44The next day Jesus decided to go to Galilee. There he met Philip, who was from Bethsaida, the home town of Andrew and Peter. Jesus said to Philip, "Come with me."

45Philip then found Nathanael and said, "We have found the one that Moses and the Prophets wrote about. He is Jesus, the son of Joseph from Nazareth."

46Nathanael asked, "Can anything good come from Nazareth?"

Philip answered, "Come and see."

47When Jesus saw Nathanael coming towards him, he said, "Here is a true descendant of our ancestor Israel.

And he isn't deceitful."

⁴⁸"How do you know me?" Nathanael asked.

Jesus answered, "Before Philip called you, I saw you under the fig tree."

⁴⁹Nathanael said, "Rabbi, you are the Son of God and the King of Israel!"

⁵⁰Jesus answered, "Did you believe me just because I said that I saw you under the fig tree? You will see something even greater. ⁵¹I tell you for certain that you will see heaven open and God's angels going up and coming down on the Son of Man."

2. JOINING JESUS

1. Finding Jesus. In Jesus' time, many Jews were waiting for a special person (called the Messiah or Christ) who was to come and save them. John the Baptist pointed Andrew and his friend to Jesus. They listened to Jesus and decided that he was this promised Messiah. What two things did Andrew do next? (41-42)

2. Found by Jesus. If a stranger came up to you and said 'Follow me', can you imagine doing this? Well that's what happened to Philip. And Nathanael's scepticism (46) changed to belief thanks to a few words (47-48). What kind of person is Jesus? That is the key question this book asks.

3. Together with Jesus. We said in our introduction that Christianity isn't for Lone Rangers. Notice in today's reading the importance of talking and being together with others. Andrew sought out Jesus with a friend (37), then he told his brother Simon the good news (41-42). Philip shared his news with his mate Nathanael (45). Faith in Jesus is hard to keep to yourself! Who could you tell about Jesus?

Prayer: Jesus you are worth following. Thank you for those who told me about you. Help me to tell others too. Amen.

discovering jesus in john's gospel

TALK TOGETHER

How did you hear about Jesus?

*discovering
jesus in
john's gospel*

(3) ¹There was a man named Nicodemus who was a
Pharisee and a Jewish leader. ²One night he went to
Jesus and said, "Sir, we know that God has sent you to
teach us. You couldn't work these miracles, unless God
was with you."

³Jesus replied, "I tell you for certain that you must be
born from above before you can see God's kingdom!"
⁴Nicodemus asked, "How can a grown man ever be
born a second time?"

JOHN 3:1-15

⁵Jesus answered:
I tell you for certain that before you can get into
God's kingdom, you must be born not only by water,
but by the Spirit. ⁶Humans give life to their children.
Yet only God's Spirit can change you into a child of
God. ⁷Don't be surprised when I say that you must
be born from above. ⁸Only God's Spirit gives new
life. The Spirit is like the wind that blows wherever it
wants to. You can hear the wind, but you don't know
where it comes from or where it is going.
⁹"How can this be?" Nicodemus asked.

¹⁰Jesus replied:
How can you be a teacher of Israel and not know
these things? ¹¹I tell you for certain that we know
what we are talking about because we have seen it
ourselves. But none of you will accept what we say.
¹²If you don't believe when I talk to you about things
on earth, how can you possibly believe if I talk to you
about things in heaven?

¹³No one has gone up to heaven except the Son of
Man, who came down from there. ¹⁴And the Son of
Man must be lifted up, just as that metal snake was
lifted up by Moses in the desert. ¹⁵Then everyone
who has faith in the Son of Man will have eternal life.

3. AN UNEXPECTED BIRTHDAY

Surprise parties are a lot of fun. Would you feel confused if you were given a surprise party and it wasn't your birthday? Nicodemus certainly was.

1. A secret visit. Nicodemus comes to see Jesus at night because he wants privacy (1-2). Many of us today still feel embarrassed to talk openly about Jesus. Notice that Jesus doesn't turn Nicodemus away — instead he gets straight to the heart of his problem (3,5).

2. A surprise birthday. Jesus tells Nicodemus that he must be born all over again. A sceptical Nicodemus scoffs, 'So do I squeeze back inside my mother's womb?' (4)

Jesus explains: everyone who wants to know God must be born of water and the Spirit (5,8). Not only must we be washed clean with water but God's Spirit must live in us (5). Through this, God changes us from the inside out and makes us ready to be with him forever. As with our first birth, it is decisive, but we grow up slowly. The important thing is to decide to get started.

TALK TOGETHER

Prayer: Lord, thank you for the new start you offer me. Please change me from the inside out and help me become the person you want me to be. Amen.

Describe in your own words how God's Spirit works in a person.

discovering jesus in
john's gospel

4 discovering
jesus in
john's gospel

16God loved the people of this world so much that he gave his only Son, so that everyone who has faith in him will have eternal life and never really die. 17God did not send his Son into the world to condemn its people. He sent him to save them! 18No one who has faith in God's Son will be condemned. But everyone who doesn't have faith in him has already been condemned for not having faith in God's only Son.

JOHN 3:16-21

19The light has come into the world, and people who do evil things are judged guilty because they love the dark more than the light. 20People who do evil hate the light and won't come to the light, because it clearly shows what they have done. 21But everyone who lives by the truth will come to the light, because they want others to know that God is really the one doing what they do.

4. A SHINING LOVE

Have you ever stumbled around in the middle of the night unable to find the light switch? How did you feel when you finally found the switch and turned it on? If you were doing something secret or wrong, how might you feel if the light was turned on?

1. A light sent in love. We don't have to look far to see the results of humanity's decision to live without God. The world is in a mess as are many relationships. God sent his Son among us to save the world from the results of living without him (17). And why? Because God loved the world (16) and did not want it condemned (17).

2. A light that drives out darkness. Think of the two examples above. In one the light is welcome, in the other it isn't. When we meet the light we have to make a choice. We can try to hide because we prefer darkness (19-20); that way we condemn ourselves. If we choose to be away from God now, we make this choice for ever. Or, because we know we've done wrong (19), we can come to Jesus trusting that he is fully able to save us (16-17). This way, we start a life with God that will continue forever. Now that's good news!

discovering jesus in john's gospel

TALK TOGETHER

Prayer: Jesus your light is too bright for me. Sometimes I just want to muddle around in the dark. Please help me to trust in you alone and to welcome your light. Amen.

What does it mean to trust Jesus?

discovering
jesus in
john's gospel

(5) ⁷⁻⁸It was midday, and after Jesus' disciples had gone into town to buy some food, a Samaritan woman came to draw water from the well.

Jesus asked her, "Would you please give me a drink of water?"

⁹"You are a Jew," she replied, "and I am a Samaritan woman. How can you ask me for a drink of water when Jews and Samaritans won't have anything to do with each other?"

JOHN 4:7-26

¹⁰Jesus answered, "You don't know what God wants to give you, and you don't know who is asking you for a drink. If you did, you would ask me for the water that gives life."

¹¹"Sir," the woman said, "you don't even have a bucket, and the well is deep. Where are you going to get this life-giving water? ¹²Our ancestor Jacob dug this well for us, and his family and animals got water from it. Are you greater than Jacob?"

¹³Jesus answered, "Everyone who drinks this water will get thirsty again. ¹⁴But no one who drinks the water I give will ever be thirsty again. The water I give is like a flowing fountain that gives eternal life."

¹⁵The woman replied, "Sir, please give me a drink of that water! Then I won't get thirsty and have to come to this well again."

¹⁶Jesus told her, "Go and bring your husband."

¹⁷⁻¹⁸The woman answered, "I haven't got a husband."

"That's right," Jesus replied, "you're telling the truth. You don't have a husband. You have already been married five times, and the man you are now living with isn't your husband."

¹⁹The woman said, "Sir, I can see that you are a prophet. ²⁰My ancestors worshipped on this mountain, but you Jews say Jerusalem is the only place to worship."

²¹Jesus said to her:

Believe me, the time is coming when you won't worship the Father either on this mountain or in Jerusalem.

²²You Samaritans don't really know the one you worship. But we Jews do know the God we worship, and by using us, God will save the world. ²³But a time is coming, and it is already here! Even now the true worshippers are being led by the Spirit to worship the Father according to the truth. These are the ones the Father is seeking to worship him. ²⁴God is Spirit, and those who worship God must be led by the Spirit to worship him according to the truth.

²⁵The woman said, "I know that the Messiah will come. He is the one we call Christ. When he comes, he will explain everything to us."

²⁶"I am that one," Jesus told her, "and I am speaking to you now."

5. WATER FOR THE THIRSTY

Are you good at conversation? Today's reading is about a woman with plenty to say, who meets more than her match in Jesus. First, some background.

- Jesus, a Jew, is in Samaritan territory, normally avoided by Jews (9).

- The woman, a Samaritan, chooses to collect water at a time when other women are indoors.

- Jesus talks with this woman, something unusual for a Jewish man to do in public (see verse 27).

This is no normal situation. Nor is the conversation that follows.

The woman's questions (9,11,12) show both cheek and curiosity. She's keeping up her end of the conversation but like many good talkers, she's not so good at listening.

She misunderstands Jesus. The life-giving water that Jesus is referring to isn't ordinary water, which eventually leaves you

5. WATER FOR THE THIRSTY cont'ed

thirsty again (13). It's quite different because it will satisfy our thirst for eternity (14). By verse 24 it is clear that Jesus is talking of the Holy Spirit. Notice also how many times Jesus offers the woman an RSVP!

Jesus probes carefully and the woman begins to let down her defenses (16-19). He knows she has slept around. She now knows he's a prophet. She tries to change the subject by asking another tricky question (20). His answer convinces her that he is the Messiah (26). To see what happens next, read John 4:27-42.

discovering jesus in john's gospel

TALK TOGETHER

How do we know when we have this living water?

Prayer: God, thank you for giving us refreshing water that never runs out. Amen.

An invitation to grow

If a new-born baby doesn't get enough food, death soon follows. So too for new Christians — each of us needs to be fed well. The same Jesus who invites us to be born again (John 3:3), also invites us to remain united to him, to love other Christians, to bear fruit in our lives, and many other things. None of this can happen unless we continue to be fed and to grow up in our faith. We can do this by:

- **Sharing ...** We all need the care and support of other Christians (and they need us as well!). You can best find this at church, or through a similar group of Christians.

- **Praying ...** You can talk to God anywhere. Prayer is a lifelong practice where we open up our intimate selves to God, pouring out both the good things and the difficult, and listening patiently for his reply. It's important to do this on our own and with a group.

- **Worshipping ...** If we love God, we tell him so. One way we do this is through the way we live, but we also need to share special times of worship with others who love God.

- **Serving...** The good news about Jesus isn't just good for me. It's good for the whole world! We need to follow Jesus' example of selfless service to the world. Unless the good news makes a difference to how we live, people will rightly wonder what's so good about it.

discovering jesus in john's gospel

- **Bible reading ...** The Bible is a book we can never stop learning from. By reading it regularly, we tap into God's plan for us and the world. Again this needs to be done both on our own and with a group.

In all of these ways, we are learning what it means to be a disciple — a follower of Jesus. As with the first disciples, we will do it best when we share the journey with others.

(6) ¹Jesus crossed Lake Galilee, which was also known as Lake Tiberias. ²A large crowd had seen him work miracles to heal the sick, and those people went with him. ³⁻⁴It was almost time for the Jewish festival of Passover, and Jesus went up a mountain with his disciples and sat down

⁵When Jesus saw the large crowd coming towards him, he asked Philip, "Where will we get enough food to feed all these people?" ⁶He said this to test Philip, since he already knew what he was going to do.

JOHN 6:1-14

⁷Philip answered, "Don't you know that it would take almost a year's wages just to buy only a little bread for each of these people?"

⁸Andrew, the brother of Simon Peter, was one of the disciples. He spoke up and said, ⁹"There's a boy here who has five small loaves of barley bread and two fish. But what good is that with all these people?"

¹⁰The ground was covered with grass, and Jesus told his disciples to have everyone sit down. About 5000 men were in the crowd. ¹¹Jesus took the bread in his hands and gave thanks to God. Then he passed the bread to the people, and he did the same with the fish, until everyone had plenty to eat.

¹²The people ate all they wanted, and Jesus told his disciples to gather up the leftovers, so that nothing would be wasted. ¹³The disciples gathered them up and filled 12 large baskets with what was left over from the five barley loaves.

¹⁴After the people had seen Jesus work this miracle, they began saying, "This must be the Prophet who is to come into the world!"

6. BREAD FOR THE HUNGRY

This miracle is usually taken as an illustration of how we should pass on the gospel to those who are 'hungry' to know God. This is not wrong but the first point of this story is that Jesus fed a crowd of hungry people.

1. Jesus cares about people's physical hunger. Some Christians think only about people's souls, and rarely give a thought about whether or not they have enough to eat. This isn't right. When people are hungry, we cannot shirk our responsibility to find ways to get food to them (5).

2. Jesus cares about the world's needy people. To calculate how many distressed people there are in the world would take an incredible number of computers. Our world is teeming with them — in city slums, huddled in refugee camps, starving in famine-stricken areas — or homeless because of war. Their needs are so vast that it looks hopeless.

3. Jesus longs for a solution to these problems. And what is the solution? For those who care, to do what they can (9), however little it may seem. Small gifts have a way of multiplying (11)!

TALK TOGETHER

Prayer: O God help me to care about the needy people in my neighbourhood and in other parts of the world. Show me practical ways I can help.

What resources has God given you to share with others?

7 ¹⁻²A man by the name of Lazarus was sick in the village of Bethany. He had two sisters, Mary and Martha. This was the same Mary who later poured perfume on the Lord's head and wiped his feet with her hair. ³The sisters sent a message to the Lord and told him that his good friend Lazarus was sick.

⁴When Jesus heard this, he said, "His sickness won't end in death. It will bring glory to God and his Son."

JOHN 11:1-16

⁵Jesus loved Martha and her sister and brother. ⁶But he stayed where he was for two more days. ⁷Then he said to his disciples, "Now we will go back to Judea."

⁸"Teacher," they said, "the people there want to stone you to death! Why do you want to go back?"

⁹Jesus answered, "Aren't there 12 hours in each day? If you walk during the day, you'll have light from the sun, and you won't stumble. ¹⁰But if you walk during the night, you will stumble, because you don't have any light." ¹¹Then he told them, "Our friend Lazarus is asleep, and I'm going there to wake him up."

¹²They replied, "Lord, if he is asleep, he will get better." ¹³Jesus really meant that Lazarus was dead, but they thought he was talking only about sleep.

¹⁴Then Jesus told them plainly, "Lazarus is dead! ¹⁵I'm glad that I wasn't there, because now you'll have a chance to put your faith in me. Let's go to him."

¹⁶Thomas, whose nickname was "Twin," said to the other disciples, "Come on. Let's go, so we can die with him."

7. WHEN TRAGEDY STRIKES

Have you ever had a dream where you are trying to run away from someone or something, but your legs won't work? You feel terror, panic and frustration. Mary and Martha must have had similar feelings. From where they stood, things looked bad!

- Their brother Lazarus was very sick (1-2)

- Jesus loved them and their brother (3,5).

- They knew Jesus could heal sickness (21,24).

- They sent urgent word to Jesus (3).

- Jesus didn't start to come for two days (6).

Sometimes bad things happen to us. And we don't always find out why. Yet Jesus never promised his followers trouble-free life. So what are we promised? Verse 4 gives a hint: 'His sickness won't end in death.' Only Jesus knew the outcome for Lazarus. He still knows best. What might Jesus have meant by verse 14?

The burning love of Jesus sometimes hurts before it can heal. When things go wrong, we must wait and trust in Jesus, assured that he loves us (5). We may not always do this patiently and without complaining (see John 11:21), but God asks us to do just this.

TALK TOGETHER

What was Jesus teaching his disciples?

Prayer: Lord Jesus, help me to see a purpose in my troubles, and, when I can't, help me to still trust you. Amen.

(8) ³²Mary went to where Jesus was. Then as soon as she saw him, she knelt at his feet and said, "Lord, if you had been here, my brother wouldn't have died."

³³When Jesus saw that Mary and the people with her were crying, he was terribly upset ³⁴and asked, "Where have you put his body?"

They replied, "Lord, come and you will see."

JOHN 11:32-44

³⁵Jesus started crying, ³⁶and the people said, "See how much he loved Lazarus."

³⁷Some of them said, "He gives sight to the blind. Why couldn't he have kept Lazarus from dying?"

³⁸Jesus was still terribly upset. So he went to the tomb, which was a cave with a stone rolled against the entrance. ³⁹Then he told the people to roll the stone away. But Martha said, "Lord, you know that Lazarus has been dead for four days, and there will be a bad smell."

⁴⁰Jesus replied, "Didn't I tell you that if you had faith, you would see the glory of God?"

⁴¹After the stone had been rolled aside, Jesus looked up towards heaven and prayed, "Father, I thank you for answering my prayer. ⁴²I know that you always answer my prayers. But I said this, so that the people here would believe that you sent me."

⁴³When Jesus had finished praying, he shouted, "Lazarus, come out!" ⁴⁴The man who had been dead came out. His hands and feet were wrapped with strips of burial cloth, and a cloth covered his face.

Jesus then told the people, "Untie him and let him go."

8. DEATH ISN'T FINAL

Lazarus has died, and the women know Jesus could have prevented it. Mary weeps and vents her anger on Jesus. 'Lord, if you'd been here, my brother wouldn't have died' (32; Martha said the same in 11:21). Jesus cried (35). Can we still doubt he was fully human after glimpsing his very human reaction captured by John in this powerful cameo portrait?

Jesus knows what is going to happen but he is still moved to tears. In the face of death we too become full of grief. Now we know Jesus has defeated death, even in our grief we can feel a sense of confidence and joy (43-44)! And we should be filled with praise to the God who listens to his son!

Lazareth eventually died again. None of us today would expect to be brought back to life like Lazarus but we can look forward to Jesus' ultimate power over death. The raising of Lazarus is a sign of this. The new life that Jesus talks about is more than a fresh start now: it will continue on after we die. As the apostle Paul quotes: 'Death! ... Where is its sting?' (1 Cor.15:55)

TALK TOGETHER

Prayer: Thank you God that death is not the end, and that Jesus can bring me safely through death into never-ending life with you. Amen.

How do you feel about death? How does today's reading help you?

23

discovering
jesus in
john's gospel

9 ¹It was before Passover, and Jesus knew that the time had come for him to leave this world and to return to the Father. He had always loved his followers in this world, and he loved them to the very end.

²Even before the evening meal started, the devil had made Judas, the son of Simon Iscariot, decide to betray Jesus.

JOHN 13:1-17

³Jesus knew that he had come from God and would go back to God. He also knew that the Father had given him complete power. ⁴So during the meal Jesus got up, removed his outer garment, and wrapped a towel around his waist. ⁵He put some water into a large bowl. Then he began washing his disciples' feet and drying them with the towel he was wearing.

⁶But when he came to Simon Peter, that disciple asked, "Lord, are you going to wash my feet?"

⁷Jesus answered, "You don't really know what I'm doing, but later you will understand."

⁸"You'll never wash my feet!" Peter replied.

"If I don't wash you," Jesus told him, "you don't really belong to me."

⁹Peter said, "Lord, don't wash just my feet. Wash my hands and my head."

¹⁰Jesus answered, "People who have bathed and are clean all over need to wash just their feet. And you, my disciples, are clean, except for one of you." ¹¹Jesus knew who would betray him. That's why he said, "except for one of you."

¹²After Jesus had washed his disciples' feet and had put his outer garment back on, he sat down again. Then he said:

Do you understand what I've done? ¹³You call me your teacher and Lord, and you should, because that is who I am. ¹⁴And if your Lord and teacher has washed your feet, you should do the same for each other. ¹⁵I have set the example, and you should do for each other exactly what I have done for you.

¹⁶I tell you for certain that servants aren't greater than their master, and messengers aren't greater than the one who sent them. ¹⁷You know these things, and God will bless you, if you do them.

9. THE HUMBLE KING

When do you do someone a favour? Most of us do it when we're feeling good. If we're a little below par, a bit depressed, or in a bad mood, forget it!

How do you think Jesus was feeling on this night? He knew what was about to happen (1-3.) What did he do anyway (5)? What was Peter's reaction (8)?

In Jesus' time shoes or sandals did nothing to keep out the dirt and dust. And Palestine had no kerbs, gutters or paved footpaths. Imagine the disciples' feet at the end of the day! Picture Jesus stripping down to his underwear, putting on a towel, and washing a row of dirty feet. This job belonged to the household slaves. No wonder Peter said no! To him Jesus was the Lord, not a slave. But Jesus insisted. He had two important things to teach the disciples.

1. 'If I don't wash you ... you don't really belong to me.' (8)
We can't wash ourselves 'clean' by our own efforts.
We must be 'cleansed' of wrongdoing by Jesus.

2. 'I have set the example.' (15) Was this only a matter of washing feet? Or was it an example of how leaders should behave? If the King of the universe serves his followers by washing their feet, then serving others should be the royal duty of all Christians.

Prayer: Lord I need a lot of help before I can be a true servant. Please help me to follow your example. Amen.

discovering jesus in john's gospel

TALK TOGETHER

Can you think of some practical ways of following Jesus' example?

(10) ¹Jesus said to his disciples, "Don't be worried! Have faith in God and have faith in me. ²There are many rooms in my Father's house. I wouldn't tell you this, unless it was true. I am going there to prepare a place for each of you. ³After I have done this, I will come back and take you with me. Then we will be together. ⁴You know the way to where I am going."

JOHN 14:1-14

⁵Thomas said, "Lord, we don't even know where you are going! How can we know the way?"

⁶"I am the way, the truth, and the life!" Jesus answered. "Without me, no one can go to the Father. ⁷If you had known me, you would have known the Father. But from now on, you do know him, and you have seen him."

⁸Philip said, "Lord, show us the Father. That's all we need."

⁹Jesus replied:

Philip, I have been with you for a long time. Don't you know who I am? If you have seen me, you have seen the Father. How can you ask me to show you the Father? ¹⁰Don't you believe that I am one with the Father and that the Father is one with me? What I say isn't said on my own. The Father who lives in me does these things.

¹¹Have faith in me when I say that the Father is one with me and that I am one with the Father. Or else have faith in me simply because of the things I do. ¹²I tell you for certain that if you have faith in me, you will do the same things that I am doing. You will do even greater things, now that I am going back to the Father. ¹³Ask me, and I will do whatever you ask. This way the Son will bring honour to the Father. ¹⁴I will do whatever you ask me to do.

10. A FAMILY LIKENESS

Sometimes people tell us we look like another member of the family. 'You're a chip off the old block', or 'You're the spitting image of your mother'. We can be like them in other ways too both good and bad! The case of Jesus, however, is without parallel.

1. One with God. Nobody has seen God, and that's why Philip asks Jesus to show them the Father (8). What evidence does Jesus give to convince his disciples that 'If you have seen me, you have seen the Father' (9)? Look at verses 10 and 11.

2. One way to God. When Jesus tells the disciples he is going to his Father's house, they are baffled. Does he mean his home town of Nazareth? Or perhaps the Temple in Jerusalem? They want to go with him, but they don't know the way. Jesus, their surprising leader, surprises them again:'I am the way...' (6).

Jesus is not only one with God (9), he is also the one way for people to find God (6). That is, Jesus shows us what God is like, and that he, Jesus, is the way back to God. And if we become a member of God's family by having faith in Jesus (12), he promises that we can start to do the sorts of things that he did (12). We will start to show a family likeness.

discovering jesus in john's gospel

TABLE TALK

Prayer: Jesus, please help me to reflect your character in all my relationships. May my life attract others to you. Amen.

How can we start showing a greater family likeness to our Father God?

discovering jesus in john's gospel

11

15Jesus said to his disciples:

If you love me, you will do as I command. 16Then I will ask the Father to send you the Holy Spirit who will help you and always be with you. 17The Spirit will show you what is true. The people of this world can't accept the Spirit, because they don't see or know him. But you know the Spirit, who is with you and will keep on living in you.

JOHN 14:15-24

18I won't leave you like orphans. I will come back to you. 19In a little while the people of this world won't be able to see me, but you will see me. And because I live, you will live. 20Then you will know that I am one with the Father. You will know that you are one with me, and I am one with you. 21If you love me, you will do what I have said, and my Father will love you. I will also love you and show you what I'm like.

22The other Judas, not Judas Iscariot, then spoke up and asked, "Lord, what do you mean by saying that you'll show us what you are like, but you won't show the people of this world?"

23Jesus replied:

If anyone loves me, they will obey me. Then my Father will love them, and we will come to them and live in them. 24But anyone who doesn't love me, won't obey me. What they have heard me say doesn't really come from me, but from the Father who sent me.

11. ON THE CHAMPION'S SIDE

Remember those school team sports where the captains picked players one at a time? Did you hope to be chosen on the same side as the best player? Jesus promises his followers that the best player of all will be on their side.

1. The threat. Things are looking a bit scary for the disciples. Jesus talks about leaving (18), and about the world not seeing him any more (19). If someone you love has died or moved far away, you'll know how they felt. But notice how tender and reassuring Jesus is as he tells them the news. Make a list of the words which show this tenderness.

2. The promise. Jesus makes a staggering promise. He will ask the Father to send them help. This helper, sometimes translated counsellor or advocate (17) is someone who supports the accused at a trial and will be just like Jesus. Just as Jesus has supported the disciples, so too will the counsellor, the Spirit (17).

3. The conditions. If you are on the champion's side, it's no good helping the opposition to win! Jesus asks his followers to show that they're on his side by obeying him. Obedience also shows that we return Jesus' tender love for us (15,21). We can't do this on our own. The great thing is that the Holy Spirit is on our side, helping us.

discovering jesus in john's gospel

TABLE TALK

Prayer: Jesus I thank you that you haven't left me alone, but that you have asked your Father to send the Spirit to live in me. Amen.

How can we know that the Counsellor is with us?

29

(12) [1]Jesus said to his disciples:

I am the true vine, and my Father is the gardener. [2]He cuts away every branch of mine that doesn't produce fruit. But he trims clean every branch that does produce fruit, so that it will produce even more fruit. [3]You are already clean because of what I have said to you.

JOHN 15:1-17

[4]Stay joined to me, and I will stay joined to you. Just as a branch can't produce fruit unless it stays joined to the vine, you can't produce fruit unless you stay joined to me. [5]I am the vine, and you are the branches. If you stay joined to me, and I stay joined to you, then you will produce lots of fruit. But you can't do anything without me. [6]If you don't stay joined to me, you will be thrown away. You will be like dry branches that are gathered up and burnt in a fire.

[7]Stay joined to me and let my teachings become part of you. Then you can pray for whatever you want, and your prayer will be answered. [8]When you become fruitful disciples of mine, my Father will be honoured. [9]I have loved you, just as my Father has loved me. So make sure that I keep on loving you. [10]If you obey me, I will keep loving you, just as my Father keeps loving me, because I have obeyed him.

[11]I have told you this to make you as completely happy as I am. [12]Now I tell you to love each other, as I have loved you. [13]The greatest way to show love for friends is to die for them. [14]And you are my friends, if you obey me. [15]Servants don't know what their master is doing, and so I don't speak to you as my servants. I speak to you as my friends, and I have told you everything that my Father has told me.

¹⁶You didn't choose me. I chose you and sent you out to produce fruit, the kind of fruit that will last. Then my Father will give you whatever you ask for in my name. ¹⁷So I command you to love each other.

12. STICKING WITH JESUS

As we grow up, we leave behind habits, ideas, even friends. But there are some things we should never grow out of.

1. How to grow. Jesus often used illustrations from nature. Here he compares himself with a vine, and his disciples with the branches (5). Branches draw all their food from the main stem. Cut from the main stem, a branch dies. So Jesus urges his friends to stay joined to him (4,5,7), and not to go their own way (6). Sometimes people say 'I went through a religious phase too', or 'religion is kid's stuff'. You may grow out of religion, but you can never grow out of Jesus!

2. How to be fruitful. Sometimes a branch fails to bear fruit. The grower then prunes the branch to force it to fruit. So too, God prunes the followers of Jesus by cutting away things in their lives which stop them from bearing fruit. It sounds painful, and sometimes it is. But the Gardener's work is guaranteed: we will 'produce lots of fruit' (5). First there will be love (Jesus' followers are to love one another, 17). Second will be obedience (10,14). It will result in complete happiness (11) that's there even when we're sad.

discovering jesus in john's gospel

TALK TOGETHER

Prayer: Lord, I'm afraid of pain, but I want to grow and be fruitful. Help me trust in you during the pain of pruning. Amen.

What do you think God might want to prune from your life?

31

(13) ¹I am telling you this to keep you from being afraid. ²You will be chased out of the Jewish meeting places. And the time will come when people will kill you and think they are doing God a favour. ³They will do these things because they don't know either the Father or me. ⁴I am saying this to you now, so that when the time comes, you will remember what I have said.

JOHN 16:1-15

I was with you at the first, and so I didn't tell you these things. ⁵But now I am going back to the Father who sent me, and none of you asks me where I am going. ⁶You are very sad from hearing all of this. ⁷But I tell you that I am going to do what is best for you. That's why I am going away. The Holy Spirit can't come to help you until I leave. But after I have gone, I will send the Spirit to you.

⁸The Spirit will come and show the people of this world the truth about sin and God's justice and the judgment. ⁹The Spirit will show them that they are wrong about sin, because they didn't have faith in me. ¹⁰They are wrong about God's justice, because I'm going to the Father, and you won't see me again. ¹¹And they are wrong about the judgment, because God has already judged the ruler of this world.

¹²I have much more to say to you, but right now it would be more than you could understand. ¹³The Spirit shows what is true and will come and guide you into the full truth. The Spirit doesn't speak on his own. He will tell you only what he has heard from me, and he will let you know what is going to happen. ¹⁴The Spirit will bring glory to me by taking my message and telling it to you. ¹⁵Everything that the Father has is mine. That is why I have said that the Spirit takes my message and tells it to you.

13. WHAT WE CAN EXPECT

Try this true/false quiz.

1. We can expect some people to treat us unkindly if we belong to Jesus.

   ☐ True ☐ False

2. If Jesus had stayed in the world, it would have been better for us.

   ☐ True ☐ False

3. The Holy Spirit will help us to understand what is happening.

   ☐ True ☐ False

If you're not sure of your answers, check these verses:
1. verse 2; 2. verse 7; 3. verse 13.

Let's look at some of this in more detail.

Our treatment. If people reject or ignore Jesus, they will never fully understand his followers. So we shouldn't be surprised to see Christians misunderstood, insulted or ridiculed. Of course sometimes we make ourselves unpopular by being judgmental or hypocritical. This isn't what Jesus has in mind.

Our help. We aren't left to handle this opposition on our own. The Holy Spirit guides and informs us (13), and he demonstrates to the world how wrong it is to reject Jesus (8-11). The apostle Paul is a vivid example of how God's Spirit is able to turn people's hearts around completely (see Acts 9:1-30). No-one can argue people into God's family, but we can pray that the Spirit will convince them!

discovering jesus in johns gospel

TALK TOGETHER

What kind of unnecessary blocks do Christians put between people with emerging faith in Jesus?

Prayer: God, help me to handle the pressure when people give me a hard time for loving you. Thank you that your Holy Spirit is here with me. Amen.

discovering jesus in
john's gospel

(14) ¹After Jesus had finished speaking to his disciples, he
looked up towards heaven and prayed:

Father, the time has come for you to bring glory to
your Son, in order that he may bring glory to you. ²And
you gave him power over all people, so that he would
give eternal life to everyone you give him. ³Eternal life is
to know you, the only true God, and to know Jesus
Christ, the one you sent. ⁴I have brought glory to you
here on earth by doing everything you gave me to do.
⁵Now, Father, give me back the glory that I had with
you before the world was created.

JOHN 17:1-19

⁶You have given me some followers from this world,
and I have shown them what you are like. They were yours,
but you gave them to me, and they have obeyed you. ⁷They
know that you gave me everything I have. ⁸I told my
followers what you told me, and they accepted it. They
know that I came from you, and they believe that you are
the one who sent me. ⁹I'm praying for them, but not for
those who belong to this world. My followers belong to
you, and I'm praying for them. ¹⁰All that I have is yours,
and all that you have is mine, and they will bring glory to me.

¹¹Holy Father, I am no longer in the world. I'm coming
to you, but my followers are still in the world. So keep
them safe by the power of the name that you have given
me. Then they will be one with each other, just as you
and I are one. ¹²While I was with them, I kept them safe
by the power you have given me. I guarded them, and not
one of them was lost, except the one who had to be lost.
This happened so that what the Scriptures say would
come true.

¹³I am on my way to you. But I say these things while
I'm still in the world, so that my followers will have the
same complete joy that I do. ¹⁴I have told them your message.
But the people of this world hate them, because they don't

34

belong to this world, just as I don't.

¹⁵Father, I don't ask you to take my followers out of the world, but keep them safe from the evil one. ¹⁶They don't belong to this world, and neither do I. ¹⁷Your word is the truth. So let this truth make them completely yours. ¹⁸I am sending them into the world, just as you sent me. ¹⁹I have given myself completely for their sake, so that they can belong completely to the truth.

14. *A* WINDOW ON ETERNITY

Very soon, Jesus will leave his friends. With this prayer he opens a window and shows them the wider plan of God for his disciples, and for the world.

1. We need protection. Jesus knows the strength of the spiritual powers that will oppose his followers. What does he do about it? (9,11) How important is prayer in your life?

2. We need knowledge. Jesus constantly revealed himself and his true nature to his followers so that they really got to know him. Unless we know Jesus, and the Father who sent him, we will not have eternal life (3,6-8).

3. We need faith. It's one thing to know Jesus. It's another thing to live on the basis of that knowledge. It's a little like trusting a doctor's prescription — you actively trust in what the doctor gives you. For John that's what faith is.

Jesus prays for the disciples — and us — with these needs in mind. 'I am sending them into the world, just as you sent me.' (18) It's tempting for Christians to hide from the world but that's the opposite of Jesus' way. He left the security of his Father's presence to come into the world to rescue us. Now we are to continue Jesus' mission to the planet. Sounds dangerous? Perhaps, but we can trust that God continues to answer Jesus' prayer of verse 15! Underline it and remember it.

Prayer: Lord, help me to follow your Son in reaching out to this world. Please give me your continuing protection. Amen.

TALK TOGETHER

In what ways are Christians tempted to hide from the world? Share personal examples.

35

15

²⁰I am not praying just for these followers. I am also praying for everyone else who will have faith because of what my followers will say about me. ²¹I want all of them to be one with each other, just as I am one with you and you are one with me. I also want them to be one with us. Then the people of this world will believe that you sent me.

JOHN 17:20-26

²²I have honoured my followers in the same way that you honoured me, in order that they may be one with each other, just as we are one. ²³I am one with them, and you are one with me, so that they may become completely one. Then this world's people will know that you sent me. They will know that you love my followers as much as you love me.

²⁴Father, I want everyone you have given me to be with me, wherever I am. Then they will see the glory that you have given me, because you loved me before the world was created. ²⁵Good Father, the people of this world don't know you. But I know you, and my followers know that you sent me. ²⁶I told them what you are like, and I will tell them even more. Then the love that you have for me will become part of them, and I will be one with them.

15. A FAMILY UNITY

Can you see how you are included in God's plan? (20) Think of the chain of people, from the disciples onwards, who have been involved in helping you to believe. But the story doesn't end there. Jesus' prayer show us that believing has ongoing results.

1. One with Jesus. The first result of believing is oneness with Jesus. This is to be like the unity between God and Jesus (23) — a family unity.

2. One with each other. Similar family unity should occur between those who love Jesus (21,23). This doesn't mean uniformity — where everyone is to be the same. Rather this unity is characterised by love (26); love that admits differences exist; love that readily forgives others. Again our supreme example is Jesus. If people followed him faithfully, we would not have the sad history of Christian fighting Christian.

3. One for the world. One with the Father and Jesus and one with each other — when this happens, the world sees the love of God in action (21), and people start to believe in Jesus. History has shown how persuasive Christian unity and love can be. Big ideals — but they are achievable. We need God's love, and we need Jesus himself to be in us (26).

TALK TOGETHER

Prayer: Jesus, we need you in our lives, so that our oneness and love may be real. Amen.

How can we better show unity with other believers?

(16) ¹When Jesus had finished praying, he and his disciples crossed the Kidron Valley and went into a garden. ²Jesus had often met there with his disciples, and Judas knew where the place was.

³⁻⁵Judas had promised to betray Jesus. So he went to the garden with some Roman soldiers and temple police, who had been sent by the chief priests and the Pharisees. They carried torches, lanterns, and weapons. Jesus already knew everything that was going to happen, but he asked, "Who are you looking for?"

They answered, "We are looking for Jesus from Nazareth!"

JOHN 18:1-11

Jesus told them, "I am Jesus!" ⁶At once they all backed away and fell to the ground.

⁷Jesus again asked, "Who are you looking for?"

"We are looking for Jesus from Nazareth," they answered.

⁸This time Jesus replied, "I have already told you that I am Jesus. If I'm the one you are looking for, let these others go. ⁹Then everything will happen, just as the Scriptures say, 'I didn't lose anyone you gave me.' "

¹⁰Simon Peter had brought along a sword. He now pulled it out and struck at the servant of the high priest. The servant's name was Malchus, and Peter cut off his right ear. ¹¹Jesus told Peter, "Put your sword away. I must drink from the cup that the Father has given me."

16. VICTORY OVER VIOLENCE

What's your reaction to violence? Today we see three different approaches.

1. Judas and the soldiers. They had already decided what to do with Jesus. If necessary, they were ready to use force to capture him (3). Their motto could well have been 'the end justifies the means'.

2. Peter. He had no plan, but in the heat of the moment he reacted with violence (10). His motto might have been 'shoot first; ask questions later'.

3. Jesus. Jesus refuses either to use or allow violence. But neither does he stand there like a block of wood! He has so much power — but look how he uses it:

- He prays before the coming crisis (1)

- He confronts the soldiers publicly (4). (They may have wanted to do their dirty work on the quiet. Jesus brings them out into the open.)

- His presence almost overpowers them (6).

- He stands up for his friends (8).

- He rebukes Peter for his violent act (11).

- He leaves the rest in God's hands (11).

Again Jesus' way seems to be the hardest. But it is the only way to overcome evil force. Suppose Jesus had chosen to respond to the threat like Rambo. Where would we be now?

Prayer: Lord I find it so easy to be like Peter, or even Judas. Please grow your love and strength in my life and help me to be more like you. Amen.

TALK TOGETHER

How do you cope with violent situations?

39

(17) ¹²The Roman officer and his men, together with the temple police, arrested Jesus and tied him up. ¹³They took him first to Annas, who was the father-in-law of Caiaphas, the high priest that year. ¹⁴This was the same Caiaphas who had told the Jewish leaders, "It's better if one person dies for the people."

JOHN 18:12-27

¹⁵Simon Peter and another disciple followed Jesus. That disciple knew the high priest, and he followed Jesus into the courtyard of the high priest's house. ¹⁶Peter stayed outside near the gate. But the other disciple came back out and spoke to the girl at the gate. She let Peter go in, ¹⁷but asked him, "Aren't you one of that man's followers?"

"No, I'm not!" Peter answered.

¹⁸It was cold, and the servants and temple police had made a charcoal fire. They were warming themselves around it, when Peter went over and stood near the fire to warm himself.

¹⁹The high priest questioned Jesus about his followers and his teaching. ²⁰But Jesus told him, "I have spoken freely in front of everyone. And I have always taught in our meeting places and in the temple, where all of our people come together. I haven't said anything in secret. ²¹Why are you questioning me? Why don't you ask the people who heard me? They know what I have said."

²²As soon as Jesus said this, one of the temple police hit him and said, "That's no way to talk to the high priest!"

²³Jesus answered, "If I have done something wrong, say so. But if not, why did you hit me?" ²⁴Jesus was still tied up, and Annas sent him to Caiaphas the high priest.

²⁵While Simon Peter was standing there warming himself, someone asked him, "Aren't you one of Jesus' followers?"

Again Peter denied it and said, "No, I'm not!"

²⁶One of the high priest's servants was there. He was a relative of the servant whose ear Peter had cut off, and he asked, "Didn't I see you in the garden with that man?"

²⁷Once more Peter denied it, and at that very moment a rooster crowed.

17. FROM BAD TO WORSE

Do you have times when things seem to go from bad to worse? This is Peter's position. His reaction to Jesus' arrest (10) shows how confused he is by events. Now soldiers have taken his master for questioning. He follows them to the house of Annas. He is allowed to enter, although questioned about who he is (17). Feeling the cold, he moves closer to the fire to warm himself (18) and is later questioned again (25,26). Contrast the way he and his master respond to questioning.

Jesus probes his questioners to see if they realise what they are doing (20-23). His answers — piercingly honest — anger his questioners (22). Yet he keeps pressing them.

Peter simply tells lies. Three times he denies that he belongs to Jesus — it is so easy to justify bending the truth. Peter must have thought it the simplest way to get these people off his back — until the rooster crowed — giving him a jolting reminder of Jesus' prediction (John 13:38). Imagine his feelings.

TALK TOGETHER

Clearly Peter's earlier mistakes led him to this. He was reckless and too sure of himself. But what about us? It's easy to sit in judgment on others' failings. Where are you in danger of failing Jesus as Peter did? What can you learn from his mistakes?

In what ways do Christians deny Jesus?
Share personal examples.

Prayer: Lord, I'm no better than Peter. Please help me to put my trust only in you. Amen.

(18) ¹Pilate gave orders for Jesus to be beaten with a whip. ²The soldiers made a crown out of thorny branches and put it on Jesus. Then they put a purple robe on him. ³They came up to him and said, "Hey, you king of the Jews!" They also hit him with their fists.

⁴Once again Pilate went out. This time he said, "I will have Jesus brought out to you again. Then you can see for yourselves that I have not found him guilty."

JOHN 19:1-16

⁵Jesus came out, wearing the crown of thorns and the purple robe. Pilate said, "Here is the man!"

⁶When the chief priests and the temple police saw him, they yelled, "Nail him to a cross! Nail him to a cross!" Pilate told them, "You take him and nail him to a cross! I don't find him guilty of anything."

⁷The crowd replied, "He claimed to be the Son of God! Our Jewish Law says that he must be put to death."

⁸When Pilate heard this, he was terrified. ⁹He went back inside and asked Jesus, "Where are you from?" But Jesus didn't answer.

¹⁰"Why won't you answer my question?" Pilate asked. "Don't you know that I have the power to let you go free or to nail you to a cross?"

¹¹Jesus replied, "If God hadn't given you the power, you couldn't do anything at all to me. But the one who handed me over to you did something even worse."

¹²Then Pilate wanted to set Jesus free. But the crowd again yelled, "If you set this man free, you are no friend of the Emperor! Anyone who claims to be a king is an enemy of the Emperor."

¹³When Pilate heard this, he brought Jesus out. Then he sat down on the judge's bench at the place known as "The Stone Pavement." In Aramaic this pavement is called "Gabbatha." ¹⁴It was about midday on the day

before Passover, and Pilate said to the crowd, "Look at your king!"

¹⁵"Kill him! Kill him!" they yelled. "Nail him to a cross!"

"So you want me to nail your king to a cross?" Pilate asked. The chief priests replied, "The Emperor is our king!"

¹⁶Then Pilate handed Jesus over to be nailed to a cross.

18. CRUCIFY, CRUCIFY!

Note the terrible contrast between this reading and the first chapter of John.

- The creator of the cosmos is flogged! (1)

- The Lord of all is crowned with thorns! (2)

- The designer of human hands is punched in the face! (3)

- The one who gave humans speech is condemned by their shouts! (6,15)

All this Jesus bears with amazing dignity. He radiates such majesty that Pilate seems genuinely in awe of him (11-12).

In contrast, the crowd acts and speaks shamefully, mindlessly shouting 'Kill him!' (15). They insist that they have no king besides Caesar (15). Humans are at their worst in a crowd. In the end Pilate allows himself to be swept along by the feelings of the mob. He respects Jesus, but fear of unpopularity stops him setting Jesus free. Refusing to stop wrong can be as bad as actually doing it.

TALK TOGETHER

Despite all this, neither Pilate nor the crowd has any power over Jesus. Jesus is aware his fate is sealed (11). He is handed over to the soldiers (16), yet even this terrible evil is not beyond the power of God.

How does the attitude of Jesus make you feel?

Prayer: Lord you know I probably would have shouted with the crowd, yet you were still willing to die for me. Help me to show that sort of love to others. Amen.

(19) Jesus was taken away, [17]and he carried his cross to a place known as "The Skull." In Aramaic this place is called "Golgotha." [18]There Jesus was nailed to the cross, and on each side of him a man was also nailed to a cross.

[19]Pilate ordered the charge against Jesus to be written on a board and put above the cross. It read, "Jesus of Nazareth, King of the Jews." [20]The words were written in Hebrew, Latin, and Greek.

JOHN 19:17-30

The place where Jesus was taken wasn't far from the city, and many of the Jewish people read the charge against him. [21]So the chief priests went to Pilate and said, "Why did you write that he is King of the Jews? You should have written, 'He claimed to be King of the Jews.' "

[22]But Pilate told them, "What is written will not be changed!"

[23]After the soldiers had nailed Jesus to the cross, they divided up his clothes into four parts, one for each of them. But his outer garment was made from a single piece of cloth, and it didn't have any seams. [24]The soldiers said to each other, "Let's not rip it apart. We'll gamble to see who gets it." This happened so that the Scriptures would come true, which say,

"They divided up my clothes
and gambled for my garments."

The soldiers then did what they had decided.

[25]Jesus' mother stood beside his cross with her sister and Mary the wife of Clopas. Mary Magdalene was standing there too. [26]When Jesus saw his mother and his favourite disciple with her, he said to his mother, "This man is now your son." [27]Then he said to the disciple, "She is now your mother." From then on, that disciple took her into his own home.

[28]Jesus knew that he had now finished his work. And in order to make the Scriptures come true, he said, "I'm

thirsty!" ²⁹A jar of cheap wine was there. Someone then soaked a sponge with the wine and held it up to Jesus' mouth on the stem of a hyssop plant. ³⁰After Jesus drank the wine, he said, "Everything is done!" He bowed his head and died.

19. IT IS FINISHED!

Imagine you are there in Jerusalem, a friend of Jesus. You stand among the yelling, pushing crowd of onlookers. Hard-faced Roman soldiers keep order with their spears. Amid the dust, sweat and uproar comes Jesus. He stumbles along under the weight of the wooden cross he carries. His face and body are bleeding from the tortures of the night. At Golgotha, soldiers bind his hands and feet to the cross with obscene skill, then, laughing, they scrabble over his clothes as if at a flea-market.

Is this the one who said 'If you've seen me, you've seen the Father'? What sort of king would suffer these taunts? The mocking sign over his head begs the same question (19). Why doesn't Jesus stop it? After all, he raised Lazarus from death.

You keep your distance as do most of the disciples — only the women who knew him well and one disciple dared to stay close (25-27). Yet you can't miss the sound of spikes hammered through flesh and bone. You feel like throwing up and wish you could pass out. Time freezes. Amid all this, Jesus' concern for his mother (26-28) touches you. Despite his life draining fast away, he still worries about others.

The end comes following his haunting words, 'Everything is done!' Words of defeat? Or strangely hopeful, as if something has been accomplished at great cost? You've lost all hope, but you will ponder their meaning often in the next few days. 'Everything is done!'

Prayer: (Make up your own prayer in response to what Jesus has done for you.)

discovering jesus in johns gospel

TALK TOGETHER

What might you have felt if you were there?

(20) discovering
jesus in
john's gospel ³¹The next day would be both a Sabbath and the Passover. It was a special day for the Jewish people, and they did not want the bodies to stay on the crosses during that day. So they asked Pilate to break the men's legs and take their bodies down. ³²The soldiers first broke the legs of the other two men who were nailed there. ³³But when they came to Jesus, they saw that he was already dead, and they didn't break his legs.

³⁴One of the soldiers stuck his spear into Jesus' side, and blood and water came out. ³⁵We know this is true, because it was told by someone who saw it happen. Now you can have faith too. ³⁶All this happened so that the Scriptures would come true, which say, "No bone of his body will be broken" ³⁷and, "They will see the one in whose side they stuck a spear."

JOHN 19:31-42

³⁸Joseph from Arimathea was one of Jesus' disciples. He had kept it secret though, because he was afraid of the Jewish leaders. But now he asked Pilate to let him have Jesus' body. Pilate gave him permission, and Joseph took it down from the cross.

³⁹Nicodemus also came with about 30 kilograms of spices made from myrrh and aloes. This was the same Nicodemus who had visited Jesus one night. ⁴⁰The two men wrapped the body in a linen cloth, together with the spices, which was how the Jewish people buried their dead. ⁴¹In the place where Jesus had been nailed to a cross, there was a garden with a tomb that had never been used. ⁴²The tomb was nearby, and since it was the time to prepare for the Sabbath, they were in a hurry to put Jesus' body there.

20. DEAD AND BURIED

The disciples may have felt numb, but arrangements still had to be made because the Jewish authorities would not allow bodies to remain on a cross on the Sabbath.

1. He had to be dead! The Romans crucified millions of people in their time. They were professionals. If someone was dying too slowly, death could be hastened by breaking their legs. (The crucified person couldn't support their body weight, and so died of asphyxiation sooner.) Jesus, however, was obviously dead already. Just to be sure, a Roman guard thrust a 2 metre lance into Jesus' side (34). Plenty of witnesses could confirm that Jesus was well and truly dead (35).

2. He had to be buried! Probably poor himself, Jesus was buried in a rich man's tomb (41-42). Joseph and Nicodemus, both secret followers of Jesus, teamed up to obtain his body. They ensured that in death, Jesus received royal treatment. The body was properly cleaned, treated with spices, wrapped in linen and buried in a new rock-cut tomb (39-40). A large rock sealed the entrance. How final it must have seemed as that rock was heaved into place! Feel for a moment their despair and hopelessness.

discovering jesus in john's gospel

TALK TOGETHER

Prayer: Jesus, you suffered torture and died for all people, including me. I love you! Amen.

Read and discuss Romans 6:6-11.

(21)

¹On Sunday morning while it was still dark, Mary Magdalene went to the tomb and saw that the stone had been rolled away from the entrance. ²She ran to Simon Peter and to Jesus' favourite disciple and said, "They have taken the Lord from the tomb! We don't know where they have put him."

JOHN 20:1-9

³Peter and the other disciple started for the tomb. ⁴They ran side by side, until the other disciple ran faster than Peter and got there first. ⁵He bent over and saw the strips of linen cloth lying inside the tomb, but he didn't go in.

⁶When Simon Peter got there, he went into the tomb and saw the strips of cloth. ⁷He also saw the piece of cloth that had been used to cover Jesus' face. It was rolled up and in a place by itself. ⁸The disciple who got there first then went into the tomb, and when he saw it, he believed. ⁹At that time Peter and the other disciple didn't know that the Scriptures said Jesus would rise to life.

21. No Body Here!

How time must have dragged on that Sabbath Saturday. The disciples, as Jews, would rest and do no work. On the following day Mary Magdelene rose before dawn to mourn at her master's tomb. Imagine her reaction when she discovered the stone rolled away from the entrance (1)!

Now time began to race. Mary ran to tell some of the men (2). They came running to the tomb (3-4). What do you imagine their first thoughts were? (Haven't we suffered enough? On top of everything, has the grave has been desecrated, or is there a body snatcher?)

But why were the expensive linen strips left behind? Why was the burial cloth neatly folded? The impetuous Peter was first into the tomb. But it was John, 'the other disciple' (3), who first started to believe (8) though he didn't yet understand (9).

We can't always understand things fully. The resurrection is so awesome that it defies our mental grasp. But like John and the other disciples, we can believe that such a person as Jesus is able to defeat death. Only this belief makes sense of the events in his extraordinary life — and in the lives of his followers ever since.

discovering jesus in john's gospel

TALK TOGETHER

Prayer: I praise you Jesus that death could not hold you. Help me to pass on to others the tremendous hope that this gives me. Amen.

How does Jesus' resurrection help you think about life and death?

10So the two of them went back to the other disciples.

11Mary Magdalene stood crying outside the tomb. She was still weeping, when she stooped down 12and saw two angels inside. They were dressed in white and were sitting where Jesus' body had been. One was at the head and the other was at the foot. 13The angels asked Mary, "Why are you crying?"

𝒥OHN 20:10-23

She answered, "They've taken away my Lord's body! I don't know where they have put him."

14As soon as Mary said this, she turned around and saw Jesus standing there. But she didn't know who he was. 15Jesus asked her, "Why are you crying? Who are you looking for?"

She thought he was the gardener and said, "Sir, if you have taken his body away, please tell me, so I can go and get him."

16Then Jesus said to her, "Mary!"

She turned and said to him, "Rabboni." The Aramaic word "Rabboni" means "Teacher."

17Jesus told her, "Don't hold on to me! I have not yet gone to the Father. But tell my disciples that I'm going to the one who is my Father and my God, as well as your Father and your God." 18Mary Magdalene then went and told the disciples that she had seen the Lord. She also told them what he had said to her.

19The disciples were afraid of the Jewish leaders, and on the evening of that same Sunday locked themselves in a room. Suddenly, Jesus appeared in the middle of the group. He greeted them 20and showed them his hands and his side. When the disciples saw the Lord, they became very happy.

²¹After Jesus had greeted them again, he said, "I'm sending you, just as the Father has sent me." ²²Then he breathed on them and said, "Receive the Holy Spirit. ²³If you forgive anyone's sins, they will be forgiven. But if you don't forgive their sins, they won't be forgiven."

22. WHAT A DIFFERENCE!

Having Jesus alive again makes a huge difference.

1. From sorrow to joy. Mary, weeping at the tomb, is the first witness to the greatest event in history! Jesus had said 'God blesses those people who grieve. They will find comfort!' (Matthew 5:4). This now comes gloriously true for Mary Magdelene. As she speaks with the stranger, she at last knows him by his voice. (See John 10:4.) She wants to cling to him (17), but Jesus sends her to share her joy with the others.

(Note that in Jewish law in those days the testimony of a female witness wasn't considered trustworthy. The fact that this encounter is written down, adds weight to its truth.)

2. From fear to peace. Jesus appears to the rest of the disciples gathered in a locked room. Their fear is still stronger than their hope. Notice what happens to that fear (19) and to their doubt and sorrow (20).

3. From inward to outward. Just as God breathed life into Adam, so Jesus now breathes new life into his followers (22). They receive the Holy Spirit, and are sent into the world just as Jesus was (21). We don't receive peace just so we'll feel good. Neither is the Spirit given just for comfort. This good news is to be spread around!

Prayer: Jesus, may I too know the lasting peace and joy of your risen presence. Help me to share these with others. Amen.

discovering jesus in john's gospel

TALK TOGETHER

What difference can Christians expect Jesus to make in their lives? Share personal experiences if you can?

discovering
jesus in
johns gospel

(23) ²⁴Although Thomas the Twin was one of the twelve disciples, he wasn't with the others when Jesus appeared to them. ²⁵So they told him, "We have seen the Lord!"

But Thomas said, "First, I must see the nail scars in his hands and touch them with my finger. I must put my hand where the spear went into his side. I won't believe unless I do this!"

JOHN 20:24-31

²⁶A week later the disciples were together again. This time, Thomas was with them. Jesus came in while the doors were still locked and stood in the middle of the group. He greeted his disciples ²⁷and said to Thomas, "Put your finger here and look at my hands! Put your hand into my side. Stop doubting and have faith!"

²⁸Thomas replied, "You are my Lord and my God!"

²⁹Jesus said, "Thomas, do you have faith because you have seen me? The people who have faith in me without seeing me are the ones who are really blessed!"

³⁰Jesus worked many other miracles for his disciples, and not all of them are written in this book. ³¹But these are written so that you will put your faith in Jesus as the Messiah and the Son of God. If you have faith in him, you will have true life.

23. UNBELIEVABLE!

1. Comfort in strange places. Reading about Jesus' disciples can give us strange comfort. Today we meet a rock-head rather like Peter, Thomas Didymus, usually called 'Doubting Thomas'. But what he expresses is stronger than doubt. He wants actual proof — he will not believe unless he can see and touch the scars and wounds (25). Does this sound familiar? Thomas receives a strong rebuke from Jesus. A literal translation of Jesus' words is 'stop being unbelieving, but be believing!', translated 'stop doubting and have faith!' (27) Thomas does this. His profession of faith (28) is a complete turnaround.

2. Believing without seeing. Are you envious of Thomas? Look again at (29). It's one of the most encouraging verses in the Bible. What does Jesus say about those who have never seen him, and yet believe? Along with countless believers down the centuries, you and I have had to rely on:

- The things that have been written (31).

- The things which have been done through the Spirit in the lives of believers (John 14:12,16).

- The Spirit in our own lives (John 16:13).

Thomas had none of these. He should have envied us! Perhaps that is why Jesus called us blessed.

discovering jesus in johns gospel

TALK TOGETHER

Prayer: Thank you Lord that I can believe without seeing. Help me when my trust in you wavers. Amen.

What would you say to those who demand truth about Jesus today?

(24) [1]Jesus later appeared to his disciples along the shore of Lake Tiberias. [2]Simon Peter, Thomas the Twin, Nathanael from Cana in Galilee, and the brothers James and John, were there, together with two other disciples. [3]Simon Peter said, "I'm going fishing!"

The others said, "We'll go with you." They went out in their boat. But they didn't catch a thing that night.

JOHN 21:1-14

[4]Early the next morning Jesus stood on the shore, but the disciples didn't realise who he was. [5]Jesus shouted, "Friends, have you caught anything?"

"No!" they answered.

[6]So he told them, "Let your net down on the right side of your boat, and you will catch some fish."

They did, and the net was so full of fish that they couldn't drag it up into the boat.

[7]Jesus' favourite disciple told Peter, "It's the Lord!" When Simon heard that it was the Lord, he put on the clothes that he had taken off while he was working. Then he jumped into the water. [8]The boat was only about 100 metres from shore. So the other disciples stayed in the boat and dragged in the net full of fish. [9]When the disciples got out of the boat, they saw some bread and a charcoal fire with fish on it. [10]Jesus told his disciples, "Bring some of the fish you just caught." [11]Simon Peter got back into the boat and dragged the net to shore. In it were 153 large fish, but still the net didn't rip.

[12]Jesus said, "Come and eat!" But none of the disciples dared ask who he was. They knew he was the Lord. [13]Jesus took the bread in his hands and gave some of it to his disciples. He did the same with the fish. [14]This was the third time that Jesus appeared to his disciples after he was raised from death.

24. I'D RATHER BE FISHING

What a strange story this is! The risen Jesus has recently appeared to the disciples. He has sent them out into the world (20:21). Yet here they are at Lake Tiberias (the Sea of Galilee), fishing, just like when they first met Jesus. It looks as if they're back at square one. Do you ever feel you're making little progress as a Christian? Take heart from what happens next.

1. Jesus meets them (4-5). The disciples weren't expecting to see Jesus, but he came to them. We don't always know when we need Jesus' special presence, but he has promised to be there when we need him. Where might you meet Jesus today?

2. Jesus teaches them (again) (6). When he first met them, Jesus told his disciples he'd help them go fishing for people (Mark 1:17). Now he has to teach them that task again. The full net (11) suggests how successful their mission can be if they keep learning from Jesus. How can we learn from Jesus today?

3. Jesus feeds them (12-13). Jesus is beautifully practical. After a night of fishing, the disciples naturally are hungry. So Jesus feeds them — hardly the actions of a ghost! How can we be fed by Jesus today?

discovering jesus in john's gospel

Prayer: Jesus meet me, teach me and feed me today and always. Amen.

Where can we meet Jesus today? How can we learn from Jesus today? How can we be fed by Jesus today?

discovering
jesus in
johns gospel
jesus in

(25)

¹⁵When Jesus and his disciples had finished eating, he asked, "Simon son of John, do you love me more than the others do?"

Simon Peter answered, "Yes, Lord, you know I do!"

"Then feed my lambs," Jesus said.

¹⁶Jesus asked a second time, "Simon son of John, do you love me?"

JOHN 21:15-25

Peter answered, "Yes, Lord, you know I love you!"

"Then take care of my sheep,"¹ Jesus told him.

¹⁷Jesus asked a third time, "Simon son of John, do you love me?"

Peter was hurt because Jesus had asked him three times if he loved him. So he told Jesus, "Lord, you know everything. You know I love you."

Jesus replied, "Feed my sheep. ¹⁸I tell you for certain that when you were a young man, you dressed yourself and went wherever you wanted to go. But when you are old, you will hold out your hands. Then others will wrap your belt around you and lead you where you don't want to go."

¹⁹Jesus said this to tell how Peter would die and bring honour to God. Then he said to Peter, "Follow me!"

²⁰Peter turned and saw Jesus' favourite disciple following them. He was the same one who had sat next to Jesus at the meal and had asked, "Lord, who is going to betray you?" ²¹When Peter saw that disciple, he asked Jesus, "Lord, what about him?"

²²Jesus answered, "What is it to you, if I want him to live until I return? You must follow." ²³So the rumour spread among the other disciples that this disciple wouldn't die. But Jesus didn't say he wouldn't die. He simply said, "What is it to you, if I want him to live until I return?"

²⁴This disciple is the one who told all of this. He wrote it

down, and we know he is telling the truth.

²⁵Jesus did many other things. If they were all written in books, I don't suppose there would be room enough in the whole world for all the books.

25. THE NEVER-ENDING STORY

When you wrong someone, it affects not only that person, but you also. Forgiveness needs to work deeply in both parties. So where does that leave Peter after his denials of Jesus? Look at what he is facing.

1. Feeding Jesus' sheep. Peter and the others have just been fed by Jesus. Now Peter faces the task of feeding those who follow Jesus (15-17).

2. Dying Jesus' death. Peter will also be taken and executed as Jesus was (18-19).

If he is to face these two things, and truly follow Jesus (19), he needs both to be forgiven by Jesus, and to forgive himself. There can be no chance of uncertainty or disloyalty. So Peter is asked three times 'Do you love me?' As in his earlier denials, he doesn't seem to realise that he is being tested.

Christians sometimes think that times of testing will be heralded by flashing warning lights. But in fact most testing comes quietly into everyday life. Thankfully so too does forgiveness. But it doesn't come cheaply. In Peter's case there is some pain (17), but also the greater gain of restored relationship with Jesus.

TALK TOGETHER

That restoration changed Peter from a frightened liar into a bold messenger. Through him, through countless thousands since, and now through you and me, the good news of Jesus goes on.

Why do you think John included this encounter in his Gospel?

Prayer: Thank you Lord that I'm part of a story that never ends. Send me out to spread that story. Amen.

MY DISCOVERIES

As you look back on reading John's Gospel, note here three or four of the best discoveries you have made as you read it through.

....

....

....

....

....

....

....

As you read the Gospel through, you may have met some bits that were puzzling or confusing. Make a note of some of these so that you can ask someone experienced in Christianity to help you deal with them.

....

....

....

....

....

....

....

SPOT THE DIFFERENCE

The Bible is different from other books in one significant way. With many books the minute you close the covers, that's it. You've finished. But with the Bible a process starts that does not finish with the reading. The Bible invites a response.

That's what John intended to happen when he wrote his Gospel.

> *Jesus worked many other miracles for his disciples, and not all of them are written in this book. But these are written so that you will put your faith in Jesus as the Messiah and the Son of God. If you have faith in him, you will have true life.*

John 20:30-31

Since John wrote this statement it has come true many, many times. Down through the years and all around the world, people have said 'yes' to John's invitation. They have taken their first steps of faith in Christ — and have kept going.

Ultimately John's invitation is God's invitation. So, what kind of RSVP do you want to send to God in response to this invitation?

You may find pages 60-62 helpful as you think about what being a Christian is all about.

Or, you may be ready to respond to God but not sure how to begin. The prayers on page 63 may get you started.

Again, you may already be on the way with Jesus, but not sure you can keep up. You will find pages 17 & 64 helpful.

Don't stop now. This is only the beginning and who can tell where it will lead?

How TO BECOME A CHRISTIAN

We have finished our exploration in John's Gospel. This is a good time to stop and ask a simple but very important question How do I become a Christian?

As mentioned above, you may have already begun your Christian life. Or, you may be nearly ready to begin and want to know how to start. We hope these three pages make it clear how you can do this.

What is a Christian?

A Christian is someone who says 'yes' to Jesus. In one sense it's as simple as that. But of course we need to know what we are saying 'yes' to. To become a Christian, you admit you need to tell God certain things about yourself and that you say 'yes' to these things:

What does it cost?

Dear God, yes, I admit that I fail to live the way you want me to. I'm sorry, and I know that I need your forgiveness.

Dear God, yes, I want to accept your gift of forgiveness, made possible because Jesus died for me.

Dear God, yes, I want your Spirit in my life to change and guide me.

Dear God, yes, want to join with all other followers of Jesus.

Dear God, yes, I want to put you first in my life. I will go wherever you want me to go and allow you to make me into the person you want me to be.

It may seem easy enough to look at this in print, and to say 'yes' to each statement. But Jesus urges us to 'sit down and work out how much it will cost' before we say 'yes' to him (Luke 14:28). Make no mistake: God's love is free. Everything God offers is free. Nothing we do can buy what God offers but it does come with a price tag — if we accept God's invitation it will have an effect on our life. So it is a good thing to stop and ask yourself: 'What will be the cost to me if I say "yes" to Jesus?' Talk it over with someone who's been a Christian for some time.

Some people put off making any decision, perhaps because they are afraid. Some common fears are included here with some answers:

'I'm afraid people will think I'm crazy.'

We all get laughed at sometimes. And it hurts. It's part of being human. You have to decide whether you love Jesus enough to be willing to take it. But of course you can do something about being made fun of — you can find out why they smile; you can try to give your point of view. Or you can try to make people see the funny side of their own beliefs.

'I don't want to give up my identity and become a carbon copy Christian.'

When you say 'yes' to Jesus, you don't give up your individuality. After all, God did make you you! Rather, you are asking God to make you into the person he always intended you to be. You may grow into a very different person, but you'll be no carbon copy.

Christians are found in every country on earth — every colour, shape, size, age and personality. They include workers, students, unemployed, rich, poor, and everything in between. They are as individual as you and me.

'I'm not good enough.'

No-one is good enough. Every follower of Jesus fails to live up to God's high standards. The secret is not in trying to be good, but in being willing to have God work in your life.

'I worry that I won't keep up.'

Sadly some people do lose their way in the Christian faith. However there are ways to keep your faith strong and growing (see 'An invitation to grow' on page 17). Remember that you aren't meant to do this on your own. We all need other Christians to help us keep on our journey. We can go on looking at the cost, our fears and many other things, but in the end each person must decide one way or the other. As Jesus said: 'If you are not on my side, you are against me' (Luke 11:23). Fence-sitting is not an option.

If you have not yet become a Christian, why not do it now? Accept the invitation and say 'yes' to new life with Jesus. If you do this, make sure you tell another Christian about what you've done.

You may find the prayers on the next page useful for making a new start with God.

Getting Started

One part of praying is telling God exactly how you feel or what is in your mind. Actually God knows what you will say before you even begin! Your own words are best. But to get you started with God these prayers may give you ideas about ways you can pray and things you might say

> *Dear God,*
>
> *I am not sure I understand much but I do want to start being connected to you. Please help me as I take some steps with you. I feel as if you are nudging me along your way and I will do my best to keep up. Please give me the help and understanding you promised. Amen*

> *Dear God,*
>
> *I feel there is some kind of gap in my life. Maybe it's because it is you I've been missing. Please come into my life to change things. Please clear out the rubbish and forgive me. Thank you for sending Jesus to show me how to live, to die for me, to forgive me and to live with me and make things new. Please take over from now. Amen.*

> *Dear Jesus,*
>
> *Thank you for what I have read about you in John's Gospel. Thank you for helping him write it. I still have questions and there are many things I don't understand. I do know that I need you. I am confident that you won't send me away or ignore me. Please make yourself known to me and help me to come to you. I need your forgiveness, your friendship and your strength. Help me to trust you with my life. Amen.*

If you need more help, talk with the person who gave you this copy of RSVP, talk to your minister or priest or contact your nearest Scripture Union office.

*N*OURISH YOUR LIFE

Scripture Union is a movement with a passion to connect contemporary gospelling with Biblical spirituality. Resources are readily available from all Scripture Union outlets and many Christian bookshops including Quarterly Bible guides with a reading for each day. Choose the one that suits you best.

Alive to God For adults who value an imaginative, thoughtful and reflective approach to the Scriptures. The reading plan offers both consecutive and thematic series. Colour pages aid meditation.

Encounter with God (formerly *Daily Notes*) For adults who want a thoughtful, in-depth approach to systematic Bible reading. A quarterly supplement suggests biblical approaches to issues facing Christians today.

Daily Bread A four year program for adults who like to read the Bible daily. Discover the practical application of its message for everyday life. To strengthen personal reading there are discussion ideas on the same themes for weekly groups.

Or, study the ***Foothold*** series of three books, each with 100 readings, which engages readers in the essentials of the Christian faith, giving them a foothold for faith. These personal devotions are suitable for use in a wide range of churches. The first, **Discovering God**, explores the teaching of the Father, Son and Spirit; **Understanding the Bible**, out-lines the main themes of the Bible; **Knowing Ourselves**, looks behind the ups and downs of life.